Francis Petrarch

Songs and Sonnets

from Laura's Lifetime

translated by Nicholas Kilmer

North Point Press
San Francisco : 1981

Some of these versions first appeared in Arion, and are re-
printed with the kind permission of the editors and of the Trus-
tees of Boston University.

For Julia

Table of Contents

vii

Introduction

I have already seen the poems offered here as translations from Petrarch causing shock and dismay to some readers for their inappropriateness, for their failure to resemble Petrarch's poems in obvious ways.

Some other attempts to bring Petrarch's poems into English verse have been disappointing because it is so difficult for the translator to avoid the tactical error of imitating Petrarch's rhetoric and ornamentation (neither of which is natural to the English language, or to a modern aesthetic) at the expense of full respect for the substantial motives of his poems.

Although Petrarch is a poet who is known to have commanded great respect, English versions of his work do not always persuade us that his poems are vehicles for thinking. When we have seen his arguments and images presented in the common light of our own tongue we have sometimes found ourselves wondering how a grown man could say such silly things.

Petrarch deserves to be valued as a real man, a careful thinker, a good poet. I have taken it as my primary aim to shape poems from my sense of Petrarch's realness, by attempting to imagine what Petrarch is thinking about and by constructing forms that will allow his thought an appropriate clarity: to make it seem inevitable that a grown man might have felt as Petrarch did, and written such poems. Of course in my versions I am making him more American than he would want to be; far more modern than he would want to be. Already in the fourteenth century he was more modern than he wanted to be.

A good deal of the impulse of modern poetry is wasteful. There is such a mystique of interest in private emotions that I believe our artists often give their secrets away until they have nothing left to give, and then either give away imagined secrets or, more honestly, discover their loss to be irreparable and admit more actively to the nature of the self-destruction they have been presiding over.

Petrarch is a confessional poet, and is responsible for helping to set us off on our current rather mad careen. But as a confessional poet Petrarch is a careful and humane moralist, a corrector rather than a complainer, a commentator rather than an exhibitionist. And for him the ritual of confession presumes the possibility of absolution.

When I was first drawn to work with Petrarch it was his moral intelligence that attracted me; his preoccupation with the fact of the various sins of self-delusion; the vividness of his psychological imagery; the startling honesty he is capable of; and the beauty of the verse that has its impulse in these qualities.

Most of the poems collected in the *Rime* were written between 1327 and 1353, and were revised, rearranged and reconsidered by the poet almost until his death at the age of seventy in 1374. The series begins in love poems, proceeds through the death of Laura, around whose name the series is composed, and ends in a hymn to the Blessed Virgin.

The poems in my selection all come from Laura's lifetime. The majority of them are love poems. They are also exercises in a moral intelligence that has as its chief aim the description and praise of solitude, and delight in and renunciation of the misdirections of love's obsessive tyranny.

Although the poems are made to be public and are completely formal, they are intimate and self-conscious as well. The kind of introspection followed in them is a development of the common Christian practice that directed a careful searching out of private failings.[1] Petrarch's publication of those failings followed the example of his confidant, mentor and alter ego, St Augustine.

Laura died of the Black Plague in 1348. Three quarters of her city of Avignon died at the same time. During that and the following years a large part of Europe died. It was after Laura's death that Petrarch began to assemble his poems into a coherent form, began to revise them, and composed the introductory sonnet in which he affirmed that he was a changed man, and that his former life was shameful: that he required pity as well as pardon.

Although he spoke slightingly of them at times he continued to work on these poems for the rest of his life. It is a testament to the power of the resurgence of old affection they inspired, as well as evidence of their confessional nature, that his revisions of them were generally done on Fridays, which were for him days of fast and penitence.[2]

In the *Secret,* the private book of meditation that Petrarch wrote midway during the first composition of the *Rime,* and long before Laura's death, the character of St Augustine, commenting on Petrarch's obsessive attachment for her, points out the self-delusion and the self-indulgence that underlie the fiction of Courtly Love; the pitfalls of greed and desire for fame; and an attendant blinding, self-congratulatory, enervating depression that seems poetic and is in fact a symptom of morbidness of the soul. Augustine emphasizes that the mortal nature of Laura makes her an unsuitable focus for the fascination of a soul that is immortal, and is designed for permanence, for the contemplation of far higher things.

Petrarch admits Laura's mortality, arguing that it is her pure and immortal soul that his eyes have led his soul to follow. She is his spiritual guide, and above reproach. It is not she who deserves reproach, Augustine answers, but rather Petrarch, his past life, and his own carnal nature which is still laboring under damaging fixations. It remains only for Petrarch to accept, as best he can, the revelation that his desire has led him close to the death of his soul.

The dilemma described here is an aesthetic one, as well as having to do with ethical and logical concerns. Petrarch had adopted the Courtly Love tradition literally and sincerely. That tradition required his amorous attachment to a woman who, because she was already married or was irrevocably chaste, was unattainable; but who at the same time, since she was above all virtuous and beautiful, should lead the poet to the contemplation of still higher beauty—the Perfect Beauty. This, being divine, was incorporeal; and being incorporeal was both absolutely beautiful and invisible. Perfect Beauty was none other than God Himself, and the virtuous life His love and care demanded. The earthly eye, however, entranced by beauty in the world, could fool the soul, misleading its attention back into the world.

Virtue, in the Augustinian sense Petrarch adopted, consisted in the choice of the spiritual over the temporal and temporary. It was the constant care of the moral philosopher to reflect on death as the most potent deterrent to sin. In a letter of 1353 Petrarch describes the experience of the sense of his own mortality. While riding to Rome he was kicked by the horse of a comrade. The wound went untended for three days until they reached Rome, at which time:

> Doctors were summoned. The bone was laid bare; it was horribly white, but it was apparently not fractured. The marks of the horse's iron shoe were perfectly clear. The odor of the neglected wound was so revolting that on my word I could hardly endure it. Although our innate familiarity with our bodies is such that we can bear in them what is repulsive in others, I never learned from any corpse the lesson of my own flesh, that man is a vile, wretched animal unless he redeems the ignobility of the body with the nobility of the soul.[3]

The event and its physical aftermath are recalled with the vividness of circumstantial detail that we expect of poets. It is a vividness of natural description that is absent from Petrarch's poetry. If, from the *Rime,* we attempt to piece together a physical description of Laura, we are left with a handful of jewelry—gold, topaz, pearl, emerald, ivory—and a few flowers. This is not poverty of descriptive power but the result of Petrarch's attempt, demanded by the moral structure of his aesthetic, to transform a mortal woman who has been made of unworthy flesh into a monument that will be as permanent as possible, and by its permanence frustrate death's argument and the continuing warnings of St Augustine. The process throws Pygmalion's story into reverse, and makes a Galatea that is to be impervious to viciousness and time.

What is ugly—"repulsive" is Petrarch's word—had no place in Petrarch's poetry. All physical things had as their common denominator chaos and corruption. Even what might appear at a given moment to be most beautiful had in its past and in its future—and therefore in its nature—the corruption inherent in its dissolution. All things existing in the world, even those exhibiting the temporary, accidental quality of beauty, have the power to mislead the soul into a deluded dependence on the illusion of the temporal.

The physical world was not to be trusted. The eye, the organ of sense that provided the strongest link between the human and the world he lived in, was not to be trusted. The work of the eye was seen to need redemption in the same way as the ignobility of the body must be redeemed, as Petrarch says, with the nobility of the soul.

These poems describe a moral quandary in a form that is foreign to us. Our poetry is carefully and obsessively circumstantial, delights in and celebrates the temporary. Our poetry uses individual moments, exactly witnessed, to sponsor echoes or implications of more general themes. Our poetry does not question the validity of the experience of our senses; rather it sometimes questions whether anything else is worth our attention. We do not tend to believe an experience is real unless we see and taste and touch it. We became cautious after centuries of being bullied by the invisible, and are suspicious that the invisible may not be real at all.

The business of invisibility is crucial since my translations swerve away from Petrarch's poems frequently in this regard. When Petrarch says (poem 71) *"O poggi, o valli, o fiumi, o selve, o campi, O testimon de la mia grave vita,"* a translator might obediently answer "O hills, o valleys, o rivers, o woods, o fields, o witnesses to my heavy life." The reader is helpless trying to find the poetry. The hills, valleys, rivers, etc., being uncontaminated by adjectives, are invisible to the naked eye of the modern reader, and as listed here are simply not available for reconstruction.

Petrarch's own sensory experience was exact. The common nouns in his poems are drawn from that experience but do not now reflect it. I have frequently taken it as my business to attempt a reconstruction of the experience, or at least a substitute for it, so that the realness of the poem will not be lost. So I translate the passage this way: "My heavy life has become part of this country; / Tamed hills, shallow rivers running through marble, / Woods and fields."

No shallow, no tamed, no marble, no running. The shallow rivers running through marble are my invention, yes—but having in mind what most of my readers will not have in memory: the sight of shallow rivers in Tuscany leaking brightly through their marble beds. Petrarch would have had in mind not only these, but also the Sorgue, rising mysteriously and powerfully out of the limestone formations of Vaucluse and running emerald green; the dirty Tiber shouldering its way through the violent pigsty that was Rome. Petrarch knew what he meant by "rivers." We, on the other hand, have to replace with something real our own impressions of the Mississippi, the Thames, the Susquehanna, the Orinoco.

In doing this I have consciously chosen to replace Petrarch's aesthetic system with another that is more trusting of the experience of the senses. I do so believing that Petrarch's aesthetic is the clothing of his moral quandary, and not that quandary itself. If wisdom is distrust of the world, that wisdom can express itself in many forms. If my translations have been at all successful Petrarch's themes of grief, hope, shame, glory and self-delusion exist in them in a clear, intimate and formal fashion.

So there are things in my English that will not be found in the Italian—additions that are suggested by Petrarch's culture if not by his text.[4] There are also things in the Italian poems that do not come into mine. I have frequently re-routed devices of personification, mythological reference, sententious exhortation, into other devices or sometimes, where I have felt that to incorporate them would weaken or obscure the principal intent of a poem, I have simply, if regretfully, left things out. The result can be alarming. In the envoy to *Canzone* XXIII, for instance, Petrarch says, "Song, I was never a cloud of gold that could fall in a precious rain, with the result that Jupiter's fire could be partly spent." The reference is to the pagan story in which Jupiter, disguised as a cloud of gold, came into the tower room where Danaë was hidden and had intercourse with her. It is plainly a different matter for me to say, as I do, "I was never a cloud of gold. God makes His love where He wills." Petrarch did not mean God; he meant Jupiter. Petrarch's Jupiter had a conceptual reality that is beyond us, which we must replace with something that calls up the passion reality requires.

The shapes and sounds of my verse do not imitate the Italian. My answer to the sonnet tends to be a small, square, sometimes irregular poem. My answer to the song is looser, more irregular, less mellifluous. My song form does not expect to benefit from the heightened reality that comes with the addition of music. Far from being sung, I expect that my poems will be read, as most are these days, by people's eyes, not by their mouths and eyes working together.

I believe the main strength of Petrarch's versification lies in his word order, which is natural, simple, direct: the word order of prose speech. Neither rhyme nor meter obscure this quality. If anything they enhance it. The poems sound like impassioned open speech. Their effect is candid, brisk and penetrating. I have felt that this quality above all others in his verse should be preserved in mine. I have tried to use a language that is formal without being precious, effetely elegant or Elizabethan in its flavor; a language that combines formality and intimacy. Because my language and my customs are not his, my poems are often at variance with the letter of his poems. My wish is to keep close to his spirit, and to respect its company.

I have been glad to have before me, in his words, the ideal Petrarch himself suggested to the translator:

> . . . that what he writes is similar, but not the very same; and the similarity, moreover, should be not like that of a painting or statue to the person represented, but rather like that of a son to a father, where there

xv

is often great difference in the features and members, and yet after all there is a shadowy something—akin to what painters call one's *air*—hovering about the face, and especially the eyes, out of which there grows a likeness that immediately, upon our beholding the child, calls the father up before us.[5]

Nicholas Kilmer

1. Writing to his brother Gherardo, Petrarch describes the sacrament of Penance as follows: "Firstly, I revealed in salutary confession the secret filth of my misdeeds, which had long been festering in stagnant silence; and I made it my custom to confess often, and thus to display the wounds of my blinded soul to the almighty Healer." *Epistolae Familiares* X, 5. (June 11, probably 1352). Morris Bishop, trans., *Letters from Petrarch* (Bloomington: Indiana University Press, 1966), p. 101.

2. "It might seem rather a curious than useful remark, that it was generally on Friday that he occupied himself with the painful labour of correction, did we not also know that it was to him a day of fast and penitence." Ugo Foscolo, *Essays on Petrarch* (London: John Murray, 1823), p. 58.

3. *Epistolae Familiares* XI, 1 (from Rome, November 3, 1350), to Giovanni Boccaccio. Bishop, *Letters from Petrarch*, pp. 103-104.

4. In *O cameretta* (poem 234), as an example, I have put, in the place of Petrarch's *vulgo*, the phrase "milkmen, civil servants, the people who sell vegetables." The word *vulgo* is a sociological and aesthetic mix, the descendant of Horace's *profanum vulgus*, which applies not to a peasant class, but to people with enough pretensions to make cultural mistakes. Petrarch's own list reads "tavern-keepers, fullers, butchers". *Epistolae Familiares* XXI, 15 (from Milan, probably June 1359), to Giovanni Boccaccio. James Harvey Robinson and Henry Winchester Rolfe, *Petrarch: The First Modern Scholar and Man of Letters* (New York: G. P. Putnam's Sons, 1899), p. 187.

5. *Epistolae Familiares* XXIII, 19 (from Pavia, October 28, 1366), to Giovanni Boccaccio. Robinson and Rolfe, *Petrarch: The First Modern Scholar and Man of Letters*, p. 290.

Francesco Petrarca lived between 1304 and 1374. A minor cleric, trained in law, entangled from his birth in the difficult political rivalries that marked both church and state in fourteenth-century Italy, Petrarch established a career as a devoted scholar, linguist, poet, diplomat and literary politician. He was remarkable in bringing to the attention of his age much that had been lost or neglected in classical culture. Perhaps equally remarkable, those poems that formed the most modest unit of his literary production, the *Rime sparse*, set a tone that was a major influence on centuries of poetry that followed.

His other poems, his letters and philosophical and critical works, are not now widely known. Much of his life reveals itself in them, in the curious kind of intimacy that analyses action and behavior without telling stories. That part of his life that arouses most curiosity, the attachment he bore for "Laura," is presented freely but with so little circumstantial evidence that the "story" itself is unknown.

It is a telling example of the distance between the *mores* of Petrarch's time and ours that the one thing we can be fairly sure of is that Laura was not the mother of Petrarch's two natural children.

Most touching in his life, and an example of his spirit, was the degree of importance he attached to having been made the poet laureate of the chaotic fragment of the ghost of the Roman Empire within which he lived. He was a fisherman also, and enjoyed tending his garden.

*Songs and Sonnets
from Laura's Lifetime*

Voi ch' ascoltate in rime sparse il suono
Di quei sospiri ond' io nudriva 'l core
In su 'l mio primo giovenile errore,
Quand' era in parte altr' uom da quel ch' i' sono:

Del vario stile, in ch' io piango e ragiono
Fra le vane speranze e 'l van dolore,
Ove sia chi per prova intenda amore,
Spero trovar pietà non che perdono.

Ma ben veggio or sí come al popol tutto
Favola fui gran tempo, onde sovente
Di me medesmo meco mi vergogno:

E del mio vaneggiar vergogna è 'l frutto,
E 'l pentersi, e 'l conoscer chiaramente
Che quanto piace al mondo è breve sogno.

1

These verses hold the sound of the grief my heart has eaten.
My life has turned the boy's mistake into a different man.
Regret and hope have drawn me into such empty sadness

My thinking makes odd shapes. Lament.
Love is known here by experience. You will hear it.
I hope to learn pity from you, not only pardon.

My name is against me: you will recognize me
As a legend. I have been that for some time.
I am shameful to myself for the same reason.

This shame is the fruit of my gibberings:
Shame, penitence, and the clear wisdom that the world's
Pleasure is a brief dream, and no pleasure.

Era il giorno ch' al sol si scoloraro
Per la pietà del suo fattore i rai,
Quando i' fui preso, e non me ne guardai,
Che i be' vostri occhi, donna, mi legaro.

Tempo non mi parea da far riparo
Contra colpi d'Amor: però m'andai
Secur, senza sospetto: onde i miei guai
Nel commune dolor s'incominciaro.

Trovommi Amor del tutto disarmato
Et aperta la via per gli occhi al core,
Che di lagrime son fatti uscio e varco.

Però, al mio parer, non li fu onore
Ferir me di saetta in quello stato,
A voi armata non mostrar pur l'arco.

3

It was the day when the sun darkened, as God
Himself vanished into death, when I was taken.
I took myself in, Madam, bound by your looking at me.

It did not seem to me a fit time to take shelter
Against the stroke of love; therefore I walked on,
Without suspicion, vulnerable—whence woe to me
Begins in our common sorrow.

Love found me altogether unarmed,
My eyes, my heart's gates, opened by tears
To give free passage toward the heart.

It was dishonorable of him to take me
Unawares in my pity;
Not to have tried his weapon on your armor.

Sí travïato è 'l folle mi' disio
A seguitar costei che 'n fuga è volta
E de' lacci d'Amor leggiera e sciolta
Vola dinanzi al lento correr mio,

Che, quanto richiamando piú l'envio
Per la secura strada, men m'ascolta;
Né mi vale spronarlo o dargli volta,
Ch' Amor per sua natura il fa restio.

E, poi che 'l fren per forza a sé raccoglie,
I' mi rimango in signoria di lui,
Che mal mio grado a morte mi trasporta;

Sol per venir al lauro onde si coglie
Acerbo frutto che le piaghe altrui,
Gustando afflige piú che non conforta.

6

I've come this far. My foolhardy desire
Follows her escape. She is airborne,
Careless. I can hear the four feet under me.

The less he listens to me the more I call,
Bawling directions, cautioning towards safe highways.
Neither spurring, nor yanking the reins, makes any difference.
Love, the need of it, makes his nature restive.

His rage keeps the bit and the rein.
I am become already a dead rider,
Bucketing about in the saddle, out of control.

He paws, stamps at the foot of the laurel.
I take its bitter fruit in my mouth. Tasting it
Makes my wounds more desperately known.

7

Se la mia vita da l'aspro tormento
Si può tanto schermire e da gli affanni,
Ch' i' veggia per vertú de gli ultimi anni,
Donna, de' be' vostri occhi, il lume spento;

E i cape' d'oro fin farsi d'argento,
E lassar le ghirlande e i verdi panni.
E 'l viso scolorir, che ne' miei danni
A'llamentar mi fa pauroso e lento;

Pur mi darà tanta baldanza Amore,
Ch'i' vi discovrirò de' mei martíri
Qua' sono stati gli anni e i giorni e l'ore:

E, se 'l tempo è contrario a i be' desiri,
Non fia ch'almen non giunga al mio dolore
Alcun soccorso di tardi sospiri.

If the fact of my living works to defend itself
From fierce torment, and from the terrible knowledge
That I will see, by virtue of the years' passing,
Madam, the light spent from your eyes,

And the hair of fine gold turn to silver,
Garlands and green vesture spent,
And the face gone pale: that in my present concern
Makes me hesitant to announce my sadness.

Yet love will give me enough boldness
That I will make my martyrdom known,
And how the years, days, the hours mark me,

Mark my desire. Even if time should fault that
My desolation will be joined quietly
By the small comfort of late weeping.

Quando fra l'altre donne ad ora ad ora
Amor vien nel bel viso di costei,
Quanto ciascuna è men bella di lei,
Tanto cresce 'l desio che m'innamora.

I' benedico il loco e 'l tempo e l'ora
Che sí alto miraron gli occhi mei,
E dico: Anima, assai ringraziar dêi,
Che fosti a tanto onor degnata allora.

Da lei ti ven l'amoroso pensero
Che, mentre 'l segui, al sommo ben t'invia,
Poco prezando quel ch' ogni uom desia:

Da lei vien l'animosa leggiadria
Ch' al ciel ti scorge per destro sentero;
Sí ch' i' vo già de la speranza altero.

13

Now and then she stands among other ladies.
Love comes into her face, and desire
Is as alive in me, as she is more beautiful than they.

There is honor in the distance my soul has travelled
Since the place, moment—they are in my mind—
When I looked upward for the first time.

What little I know of love is her gift:
My glimpse of perfect grace, and my ability
To follow it are hers; my knowledge
That what men want mostly is worthless.

I am proud of what she allows me to hope,
Her beckoning me to some distance from sin:
Light, love, air—my own soul's future.

Movesi il vecchierel canuto e bianco
Del dolce loco ov' ha sua età fornita,
E da la famigliuola sbigottita
Che vede il caro padre venir manco;

Indi, traendo poi l'antiquo fianco
Per l'estreme giornate di sua vita,
Quanto piú po col buon voler s'aita,
Rotto da gli anni e dal cammino stanco;

E viene a Roma, seguendo 'l desio,
Per mirar le sembianza di colui
Ch'ancor lassú nel ciel vedere spera.

Cosí, lasso!, tal or vo cercand'io,
Donna, quanto è possibile, in altrui
La disïata vostra forma vera.

16

The old man walks away.
He has spent his life in this quiet place.
His small family expects not to see him again.

Then, dragging his cracked body
Slowly through the last days of his life
He leans on his good will as far as he can,
Broken by the years, wearied of walking,

And comes to Rome, following his desire to stare
Once on the image of God here, before
He meets Him in heaven.

When I look at these strangers' faces, it is yours
I am looking for, Madam: desire and true pure form.

A qualunque animale alberga in terra,
Se non se alquanti c' hanno in odio il sole,
Tempo da travagliare è quanto è 'l giorno;
Ma, poi che 'l ciel accende le sue stelle,
Qual torna a casa e qual s'annida in selva,
Per aver posa al meno in fino a l'alba.

Et io, da che comincia la bella alba
A scuoter l'ombra intorno de la terra
Svegliando gli animali in ogni selva,
Non ho mai triegua di sospir col sole;
Poi, quand' io veggio fiammeggiar le stelle,
Vo lagrimando e disïando il giorno.

Quando la sera scaccia il chiaro giorno
E le tenebre nostre altrui fanno alba,
Miro pensoso le crudeli stelle
Che m' hanno fatto di sensibil terra,
E maledico il dí ch' io vidi 'l sole:
Che mi fa in vista un uom nudrito in selva.

Non credo che pascesse mai per selva
Sí aspra fera, o di notte o di giorno.
Come costei ch' i' piango a l'ombra e al sole,
E non mi stanca primo sonno od alba;
Ché, ben ch' i' sia mortal corpo di terra,
Lo mio fermo desir vien da le stelle.

Prima ch' i' torni a voi, lucenti stelle,
O tomi giú ne l'amorosa selva

Animals, living on earth,
Except those that fear sun
Light, labor as long as the day.
But as the sky lights its stars
They turn homeward, hide themselves in the forest,
Take rest until dawn.

And I, from the time bare dawn
Begins scattering shadows over the earth,
Waking the beasts in every forest,
Have no relief from grieving while the sun
Lasts. Then, when I see the stars
Flaming, I weep desiring day.

When evening drives out bright day
And our darkness clears other skies with dawn,
I look thoughtfully on the cruelty of stars
Who have made me of sensible earth.
I curse the day I first saw the sun,
Who has shown me to myself a creature of the forest.

I do not believe the forest
Has pastured so fierce a creature, night or day,
As she I mourn for, in shadow, sun.
First sleep brings me no comfort, nor does dawn.
My body is earth.
My lasting desire is of the stars.

Before I turn to you, bright stars,
Or plunge again into desire's forest

Lassando il corpo che fia trita terra,
Vedess' io in lei pietà! ch'in un sol giorno
Può ristorar molt' anni, e 'nnanzi l'alba
Puommi arricchir dal tramontar del sole.

Con lei foss' io da che si parte il sole,
E non ci vedess' altri che le stelle,
Sol una notte! e mai non fosse l'alba,
E non si transformasse in verde selva
Per uscirmi di braccia, come il giorno
Ch'Apollo la seguia qua giú per terra!

Ma io sarò sotterra in secca selva
E 'l giorno andrà pien di minute stelle
Prima ch' a sí dolce alba arrivi il sole.

And leave my body to the crumbling earth,
Let me see pity in her. Pity for just one day
Could restore these lost years; before the dawn,
Could enrich me against the setting sun.

To be with her when the sun
Goes; to be seen by none but the stars,
Only one night, and the dawn
Never come—and she not turn to the green forest
To escape my arms filled with leaves, as on the day
Apollo harried her over the shaking earth.

But I will be under earth in a dry forest,
And day will come, marked with new tiny stars,
Before so fair a dawn bears up the sun.

Nel dolce tempo de la prima etade
Che nascer vide et ancor quasi in erba
La fera voglia che per mio mal crebbe,
Perché, cantando, il duol si disacerba,
Canterò com'io vissi in libertade
Mentre Amor nel mio albergo a sdegno s'ebbe;
Poi seguirò sí come a lui ne 'ncrebbe
Troppo altamente, e che di ciò m' avenne,
Di ch'io son fatto a molta gente essempio;
Ben che 'l mio duro scempio
Sia scritto altrove sí che mille penne
Ne son già stanche, e quasi in ogni valle
Rimbombi il suon de' miei gravi sospiri,
Ch'acquistan fede a la penosa vita.
E se qui la memoria non m'aita,
Come suol fare, iscusilla i martíri
Et un penser che solo angoscia dalle
Tal, ch' ad ogni altro fa voltar le spalle
E mi face oblïar me stesso a forza;
Ché ten di me quel d'entro et io la scorza.

I' dico che dal dí che 'l primo assalto
Mi diede Amor molt' anni eran passati,
Si ch'io cangiava il giovenil aspetto;
E d'intorno al mio cor pensier gelati
Fatto avean quasi adamantino smalto
Ch' allentar non lassava il duro affetto:
Lagrima ancor non mi bagnava il petto
Né rompea il sonno, e quel che in me non era

23

In my first gentle days
I saw born and grow like grass
The wild desire that made my illness.
Because my singing makes the wound less violent,
I will sing how I lived in liberty, looked down upon;
How my neglect offended him;
What I have suffered on this account.

I have made myself an example to many.
I apologize for repeating injuries
Whose words have by now worked into the walls
Of these valleys, scrawled with broken chalk.

I have been sad. Memory does not help
Me as it used to. If this be true, blame
The sacrifice first, and the thinking that worries the wound.
I have become one single idea, fashioned of anguish.
I forget myself.
I am a cold rim around an inhabitant I have not
Been introduced to.

I say that from the day of the first mark
Love gave me, so many years have gone
My face is changed with age; thinking has closed
My heart and varnished it to an impermeable brilliance.
My pain for this reason has not slackened.
Tears will not break the surface, nor bathe
My sleep. And my sorrow being invisible,
I have thought it a miracle that sadness could show in others.

Mi pareva un miracolo in altrui.
Lasso, che son! che fui!
La vita el fin e 'l dí loda la sera.
Ché, sentendo il crudel di ch'io ragiono
In fin allor precossa di suo strale
Non essermi passato oltra la gonna,
Prese in sua scorta una possente donna
Vèr' cui poco già mai valse o vale
Ingegno o forza o dimandar perdono.
Ei duo mi trasformaro in quel ch' i' sono,
Facendomi d'uom vivo un lauro verde
Che per fredda stagion foglia non perde.

Qual mi fec'io, quando primier m'accorsi
De la trasfigurata mia persona,
E i capei vidi far di quella fronde
Di che sperato avea già lor corona,
E i piedi in ch'io mi stetti e mossi e corsi
(Com'ogni membro a l'anima risponde)
Diventar due radici sovra l'onde
Non di Peneo ma d'un piú altero fiume,
E 'n duo rami mutarsi ambe le braccia!
Ne meno ancor m'agghiaccia
L'esser coverto poi di bianche piume,
Allor che folminato e morto giacque
Il mio sperar, che troppo alto montava.
Ché, perch'io non sapea dove né quando
Me 'l ritrovasse, solo, lagrimando,
Là 've tolto mi fu, dí e notte andava
Ricercando dal lato e dentro a l'acque,
E già mai poi la mia lingua non tacque,
Mentre poteo, del suo cader maligno;
Ond' io presi col suon color d'un cigno.

What I am, what I was.
Life praises end: the day praises its evening.
The cruel being of whom I speak felt
His blade had pierced no further than the cloth,
And took a powerful lady into his following,
Against whom strength never served me, nor talent,
Asking pardon.
Both changed me into what I am,
Made of a living man a green laurel,
Evergreen.

When I first realized
The transfiguration of my person,
I saw made of my hair the branch
I had once hoped to weave a crown with;
The feet I stood on, moved, ran,
As every limb follows the soul's direction,
Become two roots over the face of proud water,
Both arms branches.

So I was stilled with terror:
Terrified no less, covered with white feathers.
My hope had climbed to the lightning's reach
And was struck dead.
I found myself alone, hopeless and weeping;
I walked day and night, searching on either side
Into the water.

My tongue has never been silent since,
While I was able to speak, of this terrible fall.
And I took the sound and color of a swan.

I wandered this bank
Wanting to speak; but singing always

Cosí lungo l'amate rive andai,
Che volendo parlar cantava sempre,
Mercé chiamando con estrania voce:
Né mai 'n sí dolci o in sí soavi tempre
Risonar seppi gli amorosi guai
Che 'l cor s'umilïasse aspro e feroce.
Qual fu a sentir, che 'l ricordar mi coce?
Ma molto piú di quel ch' è per inanzi
De la dolce ed acerba mia nemica
È bisogno ch' io dica;
Ben che sia tal ch' ogni parlare avanzi.
Questa, che col mirar gli animi fura,
M'aperse il petto, e 'l cor prese con mano,
Dicendo a me: di ciò non far parola.
Poi la rividi in altro abito sola
Tal ch'i non la conobbi, o senso umano!
Anzi le dissi 'l ver, pien di paura:
Ed ella ne l'usata sua figura
Tosto tornando fecemi, oimè lasso,
D'un quasi vivo e sbigottito sasso.

Ella parlava si turbata in vista,
Che tremar mi fea dentro a quella petra
Udendo: I' non son forse chi tu credi.
E dicea meco: Se costei mi spetra,
Nulla vita mi fia noiosa o trista:
A farmi lagrimar, signor mio, riedi.
Come, non so; pur io mossi indi i piedi,
Non altrui incolpando che me stesso,
Mezzo, tutto quel dí, tra vivo e morto.
Ma, perché 'l tempo è corto,
La penna al buon voler non può gir presso,

22

Calling for mercy with a foreign voice.
Nor could I sing with sufficient charm or care
To humble her heart out of its cruelty.

If memory is pain, then painful
The wound itself in feeling:
But there is worse to say of her delicate harm,
And I must speak, though she is beyond speaking.

She stood looking at me—let me
Tell you this—opened my chest,
Still with the look that took my balance,
And grasped my heart in her hand,
Saying to me, "Don't talk about it."

Then I saw her again, her face changed
To the point where I didn't know her,
And told her everything: told her the truth,
Terrified as I was. She turned on me
And I recognized her.
I became stone, troubled with life at the deep heart.

She spoke, her face so moved
Fear shook the stone I was, hearing her.
"I may not be what you think."
I prayed my wound to quicken me.
Life would allow me weeping;
The cultivation of a living grief, less painful.

I don't know how: my feet began moving.
I am walking still. I say little of what is in my mind.
There is not much time in the day between death and life;
So I say only the marvelous things,

Onde piú cose ne la mente scritte
Vo trapassando, e sol d'alcune parlo,
Che meraviglia fanno a chi l'ascolta.
Morte mi s'era intorno al core avolta,
Né tacendo potea di sua man trarlo
O dar soccorso a le vertuti afflitte:
Le vive voci m'erano interditte:
Ond' io gridai con carta e con inchiostro:
Non son mio, no; s' io moro, il danno è vostro.

Ben mi credea dinanzi a gli occhi suoi
D'indegno far cosí di mercé degno;
E questa spene m'avea fatto ardito:
Ma talora umiltà spegne disdegno,
Talor l'enfiamma; e ciò sepp' io da poi
Lunga stagion di tenebre vestito.
Ch' a quei preghi il mio lume era sparito;
Ed io, non ritrovando intorno intorno
Ombra di lei né pur de' suoi piedi orma,
Come uom che tra via dorma,
Gittaimi stanco sopra l'erba un giorno.
Ivi, accusando il fuggitivo raggio,
A le lagrime triste allargai 'l freno
E lasciaile cader come a lor parve:
Né già mai neve sotto al sol disparve
Com'io senti' me tutto venir meno
E farmi una fontana a piè d' un faggio.
Gran tempo umido tenni quel viaggio.
Chi udí mai d'uom vero nascer fonte?
E parlo cose manifeste e conte.

L'alma, ch' è sol da Dio fatta gentile,
Ché già d'altrui non può venir tal grazia,

24

Reserving my ill will to myself,
Reserving blame.
Death was clenched around my heart,
Nor, by silence, could I escape his hand,
Nor bring my aid to force under attack.
My living speech kept from me,
What I wrote then was written only: I am not mine.
If I die, the blame is yours.

I thought to make a fool of myself to find mercy.
My hope made me bold. But sometimes humility
Stifles disdain, sometimes enflames it.
I understood this later, in a long period when
I was wrapped in darkness. Because my prayer
Put the light out. Being in her shadow
I could see neither her shadow, nor the trace of her passing.
I lay down on the grass like a drunk who sleeps in the street.
Then, cursing the lost light, I let everything go,
Let my tears fall as they willed.
I felt myself wandering as snow in sunlight
Wanders into water; and was a fountain
At the foot of a beech tree.
For some time I made damp runnels.
Who ever heard of a man becoming a fountain?
I am that man. I am aware of what I am saying.

The soul that God has shaped
Receptive to no other's grace
Keeps its master's patience.
Therefore it will forgive those with broken hearts
Who come for mercy, eventually,
However many their offenses.
And if she waited so long, looking on Him,

Simile al suo fattor stato ritene;
Però di perdonar mai non è sazia
A chi col core e col sembiante umíle,
Dopo quantunque offese, a mercé vene;
E, se contra suo stile ella sostene
D'esser molto pregata, in lui si specchia,
E fal, perché 'l peccar piú si pavente;
Ché non ben si ripente
De l'un mal chi de l'altro s'apparecchia.
Poi che madonna da pietà commossa
Degnò mirarme e riconobbe e vide
Gir di pari la pena col peccato,
Benigna mi redusse al primo stato.
Ma nulla ha 'l mondo in ch' uom saggio si fide;
Ch' ancor poi, ripregando, i nervi e l'ossa
Mi volse in dura selce; e cosí scossa
Voce rimasi de l'antiche some,
Chiamando morte e lei sola per nome.

Spirto doglioso, errante (mi rimembra)
Per spelunche deserte e pellegrine,
Piansi molt'anni il mio sfrenato ardire,
Et ancor poi trovai di quel mal fine
E ritornai ne le terrene membra,
Credo, per piú dolor ivi sentire.
I' segui' tanto avanti il mio desire,
Ch' un dí, cacciando, sí com' io solea,
Mi mossi; e quella fera bella e cruda
In una fonte ignuda
Si stava, quando 'l sol piú forte ardea.
Io, perché d'altra vista non m'appago,
Stetti a mirarla, ond' ella ebbe vergogna;
E per farne vendetta o per celarse

So that my guilt would be better known to me, more feared,
My repentance was at fault. I raised another sin
To shield the first.

                  But she, moved with pity at this second,
Deigned to look at me, and recognized my sin
And punishment coequal; kindly
Reduced me to the man I had been.

Wisdom is distrust of the world.
For as I prayed there it was not finished.
My nerves and sinews calcified, my voice
Was driven from me, and I became that voice,
Calling on death familiarly by my first name.

I remember myself a wandering wounded spirit
Haunting caves and odd empty places.
I cried my desire unchecked for years,
Until the end of this evil came over me
And I slid back into my earthy shape;
I suppose because I could feel more pain there.

And moving my body now, still with desire,
One day, hunting—I used to hunt—
I opened trees enough to find her,
Glancing sun, wild naked, stretched in cold water.
I stood and watched while shame took over her body.
I wanted only to stand staring, not the shame.
Revenge—or she wishing to hide herself—hurled
An arc of water into my face; my whole being
Shook with it, came apart, turned animal
Stag, bayed from forest to forest, alone.
I can hear the dogs while I write this.

27

L'acqua nel viso con le man mi sparse.
Vero dirò (forse e' parrà menzogna):
Ch'i' senti' trarmi de la propria imago,
Et in un cervo solitario e vago
Di selva in selva ratto mi trasformo;
Ed ancor dé miei can fuggo lo stormo.

Canzon, i' non fu' mai quel nuvol d'oro
Che poi discese in prezïosa pioggia
Sí che 'l foco di Giove in parte spense;
Ma fui ben fiamma ch' un bel guardo accense,
E fui l'uccel che piú per l'aere poggia
Alzando lei che ne' miei detti onoro:
Né per nova figura il primo alloro
Seppi lassar, ché pur la sua dolce ombra
Ogni men bel piacer del cor mi sgombra.

I was never a cloud of gold.
God makes His love where He wills.
I am sparked flame, I am the ugly bird whose huge wings raise her.
Pleasure fades from my heart. All other figures.
I am standing alone in the shadow of that first laurel.

Giovene donna sotto un verde lauro
Vidi, piú bianca e piú fredda che neve
Non percossa dal sol molti e molt'anni;
E 'l suo parlare e 'l bel viso e le chiome
Mi piacquen sí, ch' i' l' ho dinanzi a gli occhi
Ed avrò sempre, ov' io sia, in poggio o 'n riva,

Allor saranno i miei pensieri a riva,
Che foglia verde non si trovi in lauro:
Quand' avrò queto il cor, asciutti gli occhi,
Vederem ghiacciare il foco, arder la neve.
Non ho tanti capelli in queste chiome
Quanti vorrei quel giorno attendere anni.

Ma, perché vola il tempo e fuggon gli anni
Sí ch' a la morte in un punto s'arriva
O con le brune o colle bianche chiome,
Seguirò l'ombra di quel dolce lauro
Per lo piú ardente sole e per la neve,
Fin che l'ultimo dí chiuda quest'occhi.

Non fur già mai veduti sí begli occhi
O ne la nostra etade o ne' prim' anni,
Che mi struggon cosí come 'l sol neve:
Onde procede lagrimosa riva,
Ch' Amor conduce a piè del duro lauro
C' ha i rami di diamante e d'òr le chiome.

I' temo di cangiar pria volto e chiome,
Che con vera pietà mi mostri gli occhi

A girl under a green laurel
I saw, whiter and more cold than snow
Untouched by the sun numberless years.
Her speaking, the grace of her look, her hair
So moved my pleasure, that I have them before my eyes,
Standing now on this shore.

When my thought of her reaches its last shore
Black leaves will hang on the laurel;
When my heart quiets, joy covers my eyes,
And frozen fire lives in burning snow.
I could not yet number my hair;
Nor could I count the days I would wait for such a year.

The time runs out. You see years
Vanish. Death rides against this shore,
My vigorous brown, white hair
In an instant. And I trace the shadow of the laurel
Through the sun's heat as it rides on snow,
Until the last day will close my eyes.

I never saw such gentle eyes,
In any year.
That draw me into water as the sun melts snow;
And I follow the sad shore
As love leads me to the foot of the cruel laurel,
Whose diamond branches carry golden hair.

You will not recognize my face. My hair
Will change, before pity lives in those eyes.

L'idolo mio scolpito in vivo lauro:
Che, s' al contar non erro, oggi ha sett' anni
Che sospirando vo di riva in riva
La notte e 'l giorno, al caldo ed a la neve.

Dentro pur foco e for candida neve.
Sol con questi pensier, con altre chiome,
Sempre piangendo andrò per ogni riva,
Per far forse pietà venir ne gli occhi
Di tal che nascerà dopo mill' anni;
Se tanto viver po ben cólto lauro.

L'auro e i topaci al sol sopra la neve
Vincon le bionde chiome presso a gli occhi
Che menan gli anni miei sí tosto a riva.

I have carved an idol of the green laurel.
Today is the marking of the seventh year
My walk takes me along this shore
In the bright nights, in this hot mist of snow.

Fire the core, surrounded with white snow,
Alone in these thoughts, my hair
Whitened also—I will weep on this shore,
Will make pity come to the eyes
Of some gentle person to be born a thousand years
Hence. It will be standing here still, the great laurel.

Gold topaz in sun and snow,
This bright hair conquered my eyes.
My years stand at their final shore.

Apollo, s'ancor vive il bel desio
Che t'infiammava a le tesaliche onde,
E se non hai l'amate chiome bionde,
Volgendo gli anni, già poste in oblio;

Dal pigro gelo e dal tempo aspro e rio,
Che dura quanto 'l tuo viso s' asconde,
Difendi or l'onorata e sacra fronde,
Ove tu prima e poi fu' invescat' io;

E, per vertú de l'amorosa speme
Che ti sostenne ne la vita acerba,
Di queste impressïon l'aere disgombra;

Si vedrem poi per meraviglia inseme
Seder la donna nostra sopra l'erba
E far de le sue braccia a sé stessa ombra.

Apollo, if the desire is still lithe
That inflamed you on the waves of Thessaly,
And if, with the turning years, you have not yet forgotten
The light, loved hair;

From slow frost, from the biting cruel time
That lasts as long as your face hides itself,
Defend your sacred leaf.
You were its prisoner once; therefore my companion.

By the strength that sustained
Your life in bitterness, mine,
Burn off this blackening mist.

Thus we will see through marvelous new air
Our lady seated on the grass
And shaded with the shadow of her arms.

Solo e pensoso i piú deserti campi
Vo mesurando a passi tardi e lenti;
E gli occhi porto, per fuggire, intenti,
Ove vestigio uman l'arena stampi.

Altro schermo non trovo che mi scampi
Dal manifesto accorger de le genti;
Perché ne gli atti d'allegrezza spenti
Di fuor si legge com'io dentro avampi:

Sí ch'io mi credo omai che monti e piagge
E fiumi e selve sappian di che tempre
Sia la mia vita, ch' è celata altrui.

Ma pur sí aspre vie né sí selvagge
Cercar non so, ch'Amor non venga sempre
Ragionando con meco, et io con lui.

35

I keep to myself and my thoughts,
Measuring the empty field slowly, pacing it off.
My eyes search nervously, watching for footprints
Pitted into the sand by human walking.

I have found no other baffle to shield me
From the plain perception of men.
My gestures show what I am:
Lost joy, burning. They could see it

So easily that I sense mountains have discovered me;
Rivers and woods have my sad pulse in their hands:
What is kept remote from other people.

I am aware of savagery in my search — of cruelty;
Also of my companion, Love, a little beside and
Behind me, remonstrating with me. I answer him.

Ne la stagion che 'l ciel rapido inchina
Verso occidente e che 'l dí nostro vola
A gente che di là forse l'aspetta;
Veggendosi in lontan paese sola,
La stanca vecchiarella pellegrina
Raddoppia i passi, e piú e piú s'affretta;
E poi cosí soletta
Al fin di sua giornata
Talora è consolata
D'alcun breve riposo, ov' ella oblia
La noia e 'l mal de la passata via.
Ma, lasso!, ogni dolor che 'l dí m'adduce
Cresce qual or s'invia
Per partirsi da noi l'eterna luce.

Come 'l sol volge l'enfiammate rote
Per dar luogo a la notte, onde discende
Da gli altissimi monti maggior l'ombra;
L'avaro zappador l'arme riprende,
E con parole e con alpestri note
Ogni graveza del suo petto sgombra;
E poi la mensa ingombra
Di povere vivande,
Simili a quelle ghiande
Le qua' fuggendo tutto 'l mondo onora.
Ma chi vuol si rallegri ad ora ad ora:
Ch' i' pur non ebbi ancor, non dirò lieta,

50

Evening. Our sky bends rapidly to the west
And day flies westward to the watchers.
One terrible old woman, a pilgrim, alone in a far land,
Walks more quickly, more quickly.
She is alone still at her day's end,
And is consoled a little by forgetfulness.
Evil and wound are devoured by brief rest.
When all live light fades out of our sky
My grief becomes more real.

When the sun turns its flaming wheels
To give the night some distance, greater shadows
Slide down from the highest mountains.
The farmer hoists his tools onto his shoulder
And sings sadness out of his arms,
Piles his table with wild greens;
Acorns, wooden seeds of terrible life.
We could admire him from this much distance.
One hour's change gives him such leisure.
Neither the sky's turning, nor the slow
Shifting of the planets, has brought
One restful hour to me.

Then shadows rise from the valley
Up over the mountain top, driven by the departing flame,
Stain grass and cold stream.
Cattle move drowsily in shadow like the eastern sky,

39

Ma riposata un'ora
Né per volger di ciel né di pianeta.

Quando vede 'l pastor calare i raggi
Del gran pianeta al nido ov' egli alberga
E'nbrunir le contrade d'orïente,
Drizzasi in piedi, e co l'usata verga,
Lassando l'erba e le fontane e i faggi,
Move la schiera sua soavemente;
Poi lontan da la gente,
O casetta o spelunca
Di verdi frondi ingiunca;
Ivi senza pensier s'adagia e dorme.
Ahi crudo Amor!, ma tu allor piú m' informe
A seguir d' una fera che mi strugge
La voce e i passi e l'orme,
E lei non stringi che s'appiatta e fugge.

E i naviganti in qualche chiusa valle
Gettan le membra, poi che 'l sol s'asconde,
Su 'l duro legno e sotto a l'aspre gonne.
Ma io; perché s'attuffi in mezzo l' onde
E lasci Ispagna dietro a le sue spalle
E Granata e Marrocco e le Colonne,
E gli uomini e le donne
E 'l mondo e gli animali
Acquetino i lor mali;
Fine non pongo al mio obstinato affanno;
E duolmi ch' ogni giorno arroge al danno;
Ch' i' son già, pur crescendo in questa voglia,

And their companion slowly behind them,
Urging them onward softly. With live branches
He weaves himself a hut amongst his cows,
Sleeps without thinking.
My cattle are wild, invisible,
Dangerous.

Blue water turning transparent black under them,
On their swaying wood, harbored amongst hills,
Sailors lie tumbled in their rough cloth.
Spain itself will plunge into the same sleep:
Granada, Morocco, Gibraltar,
Man and woman,
World, animal,
All ills grow quiet.
I see that my sadness has grown again during the day.
It has been ten years now.
Desire has taken over almost entirely.

I watch the oxen come back through this evening
From the patient, plowed hills,
The hard fields shaken from their shoulders.
I am in harness still to my own sadness,
Subject to sudden tears.
It is she who has become part of me,
By my doing: by my knife and hand
I have carved her weight into my heart.
Nor will her image there be moved until he who takes everything apart
Takes me. And I fear even death will betray me,
He himself not offer the rest I think is his to offer.

Ben presso al decim' anno,
Né poss' indovinar chi me ne scioglia.

E, perché un poco nel parlar mi sfogo,
Veggio la sera i buoi tornare sciolti
Da le campagne e da' solcati colli.
I miei sospiri a me perché non tolti
Quando che sia? perché no 'l grave giogo?
Perché dí e notte gli occhi miei son molli?
Misero me! che volli,
Quando primier sí fiso
Gli tenni nel bel viso,
Per iscolpirlo, imaginando, in parte
Onde mai né per forza né per arte
Mosso sarà, fin ch' i' sia dato in preda
A chi tutto diparte?
Né so ben anco che di lei mi creda.

Canzon, se l'esser meco
Dal mattino a la sera
T' ha fatto di mia schiera,
Tu non vorrai mostrarti in ciascun loco:
E d'altrui loda curerai sí poco,
Ch'assai ti fia pensar di poggio in poggio
Come m'ha concio 'l foco
Di questa viva petra ov'io m'appoggio.

You are my flock and cattle; that should be some comfort.
Morning to evening you move secretly here like strange beasts.
You know the principle of life within this stone,
The wound left by a great flame, wrapped in shadow.

52

Non al suo amante piú Dïana piacque
Quando, per tal ventura, tutta ignuda
La vide in mezzo de le gelide acque;

Ch' a me la pastorella alpestra e cruda
Posta a bagnar un leggiadretto velo
Ch' a l'aura il vago e biondo capel chiuda;

Tal che mi fece, or quand' egli arde il cielo,
Tutto tremar d' un amoroso gelo.

Diana did not please her lover more
When by some chance quite naked
He saw her standing in cold water,

Than the wild hill girl,
Washing a light cloth in the bright air,
Pleased me.

The sky is burning. I am shaking with cold.

Per ch' al viso d'Amor portava insegna,
Mosse una pellegrina il mio cor vano;
Ch' ogni altra mi parea d'onor men degna.

E lei seguendo su per l'erbe verdi
Udii dir alta voce di lontano:
Ahi quanti passi per la selva perdi!

Allor mi strinsi a l'ombra d'un bel faggio,
Tutto pensoso; e rimirando intorno
Vidi assai periglioso il mio vïaggio;

E tornai 'n dietro quasi a mezzo il giorno.

Because she carried love's mark in her face
A pilgrim woman moved my desire.
Any other thing seemed less worthy of honor.

And following her over the green grass
I heard speak a high voice from the distance,
"Oheeie! How many steps lost in these woods!"

Then I paused in the shadow of a beech tree
Quite thoughtful; and looking again around
I saw my wandering was dangerous.

I turned back again almost at noon.

Perché la vita è breve
E l'ingegno paventa a l'alta impresa,
Né di lui né di lei molto mi fido;
Ma spero che sia intesa
Là dov' io bramo e là dov' esser deve
La doglia mia, la qual tacendo i' grido.
Occhi leggiadri dov'Amor fa nido,
A voi rivolgo il mio debile stile
Pigro da sé, ma 'l gran piacer lo sprona:
E chi di voi ragiona
Tien dal suggetto un abito gentile,
Che con l' ale amorose
Levando il parte d'ogni pensier vile:
Con queste alzato vengo a dire or cose,
C' ho portate nel cor gran tempo ascose.

Non perch'io non m'aveggia
Quanto mia laude è ingiurïosa a voi,
Ma contrastar non posso al gran desio
Lo quale è in me, da poi
Ch' i' vidi quel che pensier non pareggia
Non che l'aguagli altrui parlar o mio.
Principio del mio dolce stato rio,
Altri che voi so ben che non m'intende.
Quando a gli ardenti rai neve divegno,
Vostro gentile sdegno
Forse ch' allor mia indegnitate offende.
Oh, se questa temenza
Non temprasse l'arsura che m' incende,

Lifetime is cut off
Short. My intelligence, my strength of invention,
Are held in abeyance by fear of the task's size.
I have never put faith in life; nor will I trust
My genius much any more.
I hope you can hear what I say
Because my grief should be known. Otherwise
I announce it only foolishly.
The shape of your face is in my mind.
It is to you I have been speaking all this time,
Slowly, but driven by an intense delight.
And you will sense my soul purged of all vileness
Speaking as it does here, in this high form;
And this after having been locked away so many years,
This purity remaining, should do my love some credit.

I am aware of the hurt this can be to you.
My speaking now is not mine to resist.
What I have seen of you is greater than my invention
Could be; and even if thinking of it denies all tact,
It is my beginning. This event has made me
What I am: strong bitterness existing in your light
With the gentleness of water.

Beato venir men! che 'n lor presenza
M'è piú caro il morir, che 'l viver senza.

Dunque, ch' i' non mi sfaccia,
Sí frale oggetto a sí possente foco,
Non è proprio valor che me ne scampi;
Ma la paura un poco,
Che 'l sangue vago per le vene agghiaccia,
Risalda 'l cor, perché piú tempo avampi.
O poggi, o valli, o fiumi, o selve, o campi,
O testimon de la mia grave vita;
Quante volte m'udiste chiamar morte!
Ahi dolorosa sorte!
Lo star mi strugge, e 'l fuggir non m'aita.
Ma, se maggior paura
Non m'affrenasse, via corta e spedita
Trarrebbe a fin quest'aspra pena e dura;
E la colpa è di tal che non ha cura.

Dolor, perché mi meni
Fuor di camin a dir quel ch' i' non voglio?
Sostien ch' io vada ove 'l piacer mi spigne.
Già di voi non mi doglio,
Occhi sopra 'l mortal corso sereni,
Né di lui ch' a tal nodo mi distrigne.
Vedete ben quanti color depigne
Amor sovente in mezzo del mio volto,
E potrete pensar qual dentro fammi,
Là 've dí e notte stammi
A dosso col poder c' ha in voi raccolto,
Luci beate e liete,
Se non che 'l veder voi stesse v' è tolto

And it is only you who could possibly understand this.
You show some scorn for my being humbled.
It is fear that halts me — and you are that fear's master.
Were you to exercise your preserve, you would discover
My death easily in an instant.

My preservation is not the act of my will.
I am the fluttering object of great flame, my own desire.
The fear that collects in a tight fist of cold
Around my heart, is what preserves me.
Desire halts in the vein
So that it burns more slowly.

My heavy life has become part of this country;
Tamed hills, shallow rivers running through marble,
Woods and fields — all beckon death with my voice.
I say that one shocking pain followed by quiet
Would come graciously, were I not so fearful.
Such act would echo your carelessness.

My pardon: I fear sorrow has led me to say
Things I meant not to: I was going to think about you.
If you could see the fact of your beauty
As love carves it into my brain, you would realize
The agony that keeps me wakeful.

Ma quante volte a me vi rivolgete
Conoscete in altrui quel che voi sete.

S' a voi fosse sí nota
La divina incredibile bellezza
Di ch' io ragiono, come a chi la mira,
Misurata allegrezza
Non avria 'l cor; però forse è remota
Dal vigor natural che v'apre e gira.
Felice l'alma che per voi sospira,
Lumi del ciel; per li quali io ringrazio
La vita che per altro non m'è a grado.
Oi me, perché sí rado
Mi date quel dond'io mai non son sazio?
Perché non piú sovente
Mirate qual Amor di me fa strazio?
E perché mi spogliate immantenente
Del ben che ad ora ad or l'anima sente?

Dico, ch' ad ora ad ora,
Vostra mercede, i' sento in mezzo l'alma
Una dolcezza inusitata e nova;
La qual ogni altra salma
Di noiosi pensier disgombra allora
Sí, che di mille un sol vi si ritrova:
Quel tanto a me, non piú, del viver giova.
E, se questo mio ben durasse alquanto,
Nullo stato aguagliarse al mio potrebbe:
Ma forse altrui farebbe
Invido, e me superbo, l'onor tanto:
Però, lasso! conviensi,
Che l'estremo del riso assaglia il pianto,

Light: you are all light. Your radiance
Stands around you like a wall, reflecting
Yourself back to you surely,
If you look at me.

There should be gladness in your heart at that incredible
Vision, as there is a sort of gladness here,
My knowing the fact of my desire, and its object's
Clear beauty. Is it still simply you I am calling
By death's name? Life. Sky light.

So there is mercy in your regard.
I feel some distant gentleness in my soul,
Some place unwounded—just so much life-liking.
Were this joy to grow, I would become happier
Than anything I have imagined ever, and weep . . .

My weeping clears my eyes, then.
I see I am where I began.

E 'nterrompendo quelli spirti accensi
A me ritorni, e di me stesso pensi.

L'amoroso pensero
Ch' alberga dentro, in voi mi si discopre
Tal, che mi trae del cor ogni altra gioia:
Onde parole et opre
Escon di me sí fatte allor, ch' i' spero
Farmi immortal, perché la carne moia.
Fugge al vostro apparir angoscia e noia,
E nel vostro partir tornano insieme.
Ma, perché la memoria innamorata
Chiude lor poi l'entrata,
Di là non vanno da le parti estreme.
Onde, s' alcun bel frutto
Nasce di me, da voi vien prima il seme:
Io per me son quasi un terreno asciutto
Cólto da voi; e 'l pregio è vostro in tutto.

Canzon, tu non m'acqueti, anzi m'infiammi
A dir di quel ch' a me stesso m'invola:
Però sia certa di non esser sola.

I see Love again as the joyless caged beast
Living within me.
If anything live after my death, it will be this
Raw anguish, who is assuaged only when looking at you
Directly, speaking of you.
I am myself already dry earth,
Cultivated by you to nurture such foreign growth.

The song will not appease me, but make flame
Crawl from my centre and steal into air as singing.
As singing, it will not exist in isolation.

81

Io son sí stanco sotto il fascio antico
De le mie colpe e de l'usanza ria,
Ch' i' temo forte di mancar tra via
E di cader in man del mio nemico.

Ben venne a dilivrarmi un grande amico,
Per somma et ineffabil cortesia;
Poi volò fuor de la veduta mia
Sí ch' a mirarlo indarno m'affatico.

Ma la sua voce ancor qua giú rimbomba
— O voi che travagliate, ecco 'l camino:
Venite a me, se 'l passo altri non serra. —

Qual grazia, qual amore, o qual destino
Mi darà penne in guisa di colomba,
Ch' i' mi riposi e levimi da terra?

I was so wearied under the ancient burden
Of my sins, and of habitual evils,
That I feared much to fall by the wayside,
And to come into the hands of my enemy.

Then a friend came to deliver me
By his great and unspeakable courtesy;
But he vanished beyond my sight
So that I weary myself in vain now, looking for him.

His voice is clear to me still:
"You who are laboring, this
Is the way. Come to me when you have the freedom."

What grace, what love or destiny
Will give me a dove's wings
So that after my rest I may take myself into the sky?

La bella donna che cotanto amavi
Subitamente s' è da noi partita,
E, per quel ch' io ne speri, al ciel salita,
Sí furon gli atti suoi dolci, soavi.

Tempo è da ricovrare ambe le chiavi
Del tuo cor, ch' ella possedeva in vita
E seguir lei per via dritta e spedita:
Peso terren non sia piú che t'aggravi.

Poi che se' sgombro de la maggior salma,
L'altre puoi giuso agevolmente porre,
Salendo quasi un pellegrino scarco.

Ben vedi omai sí come a morte corre
Ogni cosa creata e quanto a l'alma
Bisogna ir lieve al periglioso varco.

91

The lady whom you have loved so deeply
Has left us without warning.
So kind and gentle were her actions, I must
Think her in heaven.

While she lived, she held both keys to your heart.
It is time to recover them, and to follow her.
Strip the world's weight from you.

The first great chain being broken,
Others will fall with ease.
You will be a pilgrim, and weightless.

You have seen everything created running toward its death.
The soul must keep poverty for the dangerous journey.

Cesare, poi che 'l traditor d' Egitto
Li fece il don de l'onorata testa,
Celando l'allegrezza manifesta,
Pianse per gli occhi fuor, sí come è scritto;

Ed Anibàl, quando a l'imperio afflitto
Vide farsi fortuna sí molesta,
Rise fra gente lagrimosa e mesta,
Per isfogare il suo acerbo despitto;

E cosí aven che l'animo ciascuna
Sua passïon sotto 'l contrario manto
Ricopre con la vista or chiara or bruna:

Però, s' alcuna volta i' rido o canto,
Faccio 'l perch' i' non ho se non quest'una
Via da celare il mio angoscioso pianto.

102

When Egypt's betrayer handed Caesar, as a gift,
The adorned cut head, Caesar wept.
His joy was evident.

And Hannibal, surrounded by tear-stricken people,
Laughed while he witnessed the dissolution of his empire,
Mocking the bitterness of his loss.

The cloak that hides the soul
Shows it, therefore,
Be the face grim or gentle.

If I laugh sometimes, and sing,
It is because I have no other hiding place.

109

Lasso, quante fïate Amor m'assale,
Che fra la notte e 'l dí son piú di mille,
Torno dov' arder vidi le faville
Che 'l foco del mio cor fanno immortale.

Ivi m'acqueto: e son condotto a tale,
Ch' a nona, a vespro, a l'alba ed a le squille
Le trovo nel pensier tanto tranquille
Che di null'altro mi rimembra o cale.

L'aura soave che dal chiaro viso
Move co 'l suon de le parole accorte
Per far dolce sereno ovunque spira,

Quasi un spirto gentil di paradiso
Sempre in quell'aere par che mi conforte;
Sí che 'l cor lasso altrove non respira.

109

When love brings pain,
Frequently enough,
I turn to the place where the spark
Struck fire into my soul forever.

I become calm. I am quieted to the extent
That I find tranquility in my thoughts for hours at a time.
I remember nothing else. I mind nothing.

Wind moving away from her clear image
Makes shrewd words and bright quiet air.

It seems a blessed soul there to comfort me always,
So that my heart speaks cleanly from its pain.

Perseguendomi Amor al luogo usato
Ristretto in guisa d'uom ch' aspetta guerra
Che si provede e i passi intorno serra,
De' miei antichi pensier mi stava armato.

Volsimi; e vidi un'ombra che da lato
Stampava il sole, e riconobbi in terra
Quella che, se 'l giudicio mio non erra,
Era piú degna d'immortale stato.

I' dicea fra mio cor: Perché paventi?
Ma non fu prima dentro il penser giunto,
Che i raggi ov' io mi struggo eran presenti.

Come co 'l balenar tona in un punto,
Cosí fu' io da' begli occhi lucenti
E d'un dolce saluto inseme aggiunto.

110

I say it again; I was armed and alert,
Ready for war, walking dangerously,
My old convictions drawn around me.

A shadow a woman's form crossed the sun
Over the land. I turned, recognized
Both her, and my desire that she be preserved.

Fear came, whose cause I was too slow
To guess. The thought shattered and vanished in
Violent light that blinds me still,

As lightning strikes thunder.
And she greeted me.

Pien di quella ineffabile dolcezza
Che del bel viso trassen gli occhi miei
Nel dí che volentier chiusi gli avrei
Per non mirar già mai minor bellezza,

Lassai quel ch' i' piú bramo; et ho sí avezza
La mente a contemplar sola costei,
Ch' altro non vede, e ciò che non è lei
Già per antica usanza odia e disprezza.

In una valle chiusa d'ogni 'ntorno,
Ch' è refrigerio de' sospir miei lassi,
Giunsi sol con Amor, pensoso e tardo.

Ivi non donne, ma fontane e sassi,
E l'imagine trovo di quel giorno
Che 'l pensier mio figura ovunqu' io sguardo.

116

I had taken in such unspeakable sweetness
From her face, I wanted to lock my eyes,
To see nothing beautiful any more.

What I desired, I kept out. And I have held my mind
So narrowly to contemplate her, I see nothing else.
What is not hers, by ancient custom, brings my contempt.

This closed valley comforts my wasted breathing.
I am alone with love here; able to think slowly.

There are no women. Fountains and stones.
I cast the shadow of that day in front of me, walking.

Rimansi a dietro il sestodecim' anno
De' miei sospiri, et io trapasso inanzi
Verso l'estremo; e parmi che pur dianzi
Fosse 'l principio di cotanto affanno.

L'amar m'è dolce, et util il mio danno,
E 'l viver grave; e prego ch' egli avanzi
L'empia fortuna, e temo non chiuda anzi
Morte i begli occhi che parlar mi fanno.

Or qui son, lasso, e voglio esser altrove,
E vorrei piú volere, e piú non voglio,
E per piú non poter fo quant' io posso;

E d'antichi desir lagrime nove
Provan com' io son pur quel ch' i' mi soglio,
Né per mille rivolte ancor son mosso.

118

I am walking toward the end of something.
I have just passed my sixteenth year of sadness.
The first day of pain feels as near as it ever did.

I have grown to depend on futile desire.
Life is uneasy in me. I pray that I outlive
My grief. I fear death's closing the eyes I speak of.

I am in place. I would move to another country.
I do what a person can who wants nothing.

New blood speaks from the old wound,
Rising again after so many holdings back.
I am what I was. I have not moved.

Una donna piú bella assai che 'l sole
E piú lucente, e d'altr' e tanta etade,
Con famosa beltade,
Acerbo ancor, mi trasse a la sua schiera.
Questa in penseri in opre et in parole
(Però ch' è de le cose al mondo rade),
Questa per mille strade
Sempre inanzi mi fu, leggiadra, altera.
Solo per lei tornai da quel ch'i' era,
Poi ch' i' soffersi gli occhi suoi da presso:
Per suo amor m' er' io messo
A faticosa impresa assai per tempo;
Tal che, s' i' arrivo al desïato porto,
Spero per lei gran tempo
Viver, quand' altri mi terrà per morto.

Questa mia donna mi menò molt'anni
Pien di vaghezza giovenile ardendo,
Si come ora io comprendo,
Sol per aver di me piú certa prova,
Mostrandomi pur l'ombra o 'l velo o' panni
Tal or di sé, ma 'l viso nascondendo:
Et io, lasso, credendo
Vederne assai, tutta l'età mia nova
Passai contento; e 'l rimembrar mi giova.
Poi ch' alquanto di lei veggi' or piú inanzi,
I' dico che pur dianzi,
Qual io non l'avea vista in fin allora,
Mi si scoverse: onde mi nacque un ghiaccio

A lady lovelier than sunlight,
And brighter and of equally great age
Drew me, still green, into her company.
It was her beauty first that beckoned
Me—she of the world's most rare—
The thousand graces of her thought,
Speech, her actions, stood before me
Always, proud and radiant beacons.
It was on her behalf I changed from what I had been,
Allowing her regard to approach me;
Because I loved her, I was myself
For a long time engaged in a fatiguing enterprise.
There will be an end to it. I hope to live
Through her influence for a long time
After the people think me dead.

This lady led me many years,
Led the heat of my young man's desire,
To take, as I understand only now,
More certain proof of me,
Showing me her shadow, her veil or clothing
Sometimes, she kept her face from me;
And I, believing myself content with what I saw,
Made no outcry through my early time.
That cry might appear now as laughter
In my memory. For I see much of her.
It is just now she has discovered
So much of herself to me, memory slides into the background.
She has struck me with knowledge

Nel core; et evvi ancora
E sarà sempre fin ch' i' le sia in braccio.

Ma non me 'l tolse la paura o 'l gelo
Che pur tanta baldanza al mio cor diedi,
Ch' i' le mi strinsi a' piedi
Per piú dolcezza trar de gli occhi suoi:
Et ella, che remosso avea già il velo
Di nanzi a' miei, mi disse — Amico, or vedi
Com'io son bella; e chiedi
Quanto par si convenga a gli anni tuoi. —
— Madonna, dissi, già gran tempo in voi
Posi 'l mio amor, ch' i' sento or sí 'nfiammato:
Ond' a me in questo stato
Altro volere o disvoler m'è tolto. —
Con voce allor di sí mirabil tempre
Rispose, e con un volto
Che temer e sperar mi farà sempre:

— Rado fu al mondo fra cosí gran turba
Ch' udendo ragionar del mio valore
Non si sentisse al core
Per breve tempo al men qualche favilla:
Ma l'adversaria mia che 'l ben perturba
Tosto la spegne: ond' ogni vertú more,
E regna altro signore
Che promette una vita piú tranquilla.
De la tua mente Amor, che prima aprilla,
Mi dice cose veramente, ond' io
Veggio che 'l gran desio
Pur d'onorato fin ti farà degno;

In a coldness that takes my heart.
I can feel the fingers of ice now, and will until
I am in her arms; her arms surround me.

Yet even breathless pain did not prevent
My reaching to embrace her feet.
I wanted to make her eyes show that they knew me;
Because I saw her clearly.
She said, "You have seen now that I am beautiful.
What price do you ask me for your years of service?"
"My lady," I said, "You have taken
My power to desire, or to cease desiring."
Her voice and countenance remained gentle
And distant. Fear and hope struggled in me.

"There has seldom been a man in these crowds
Who hearing talk of my authority
Did not feel a certain flicker of love
For a little time. It is lost easily
Almost always. Another master
Moves in, promising a more tranquil life.
Love, who has opened your mind, has told me of it
So that I see your great desire,
And that a noble end will come of it.
You are one of my few friends. I give you
This sign, therefore—a lady
Lovelier to look at than myself."
I wanted to say it was impossible,
Began to speak, when she demanded
That my look follow hers. "Look there,
A woman who has shown herself almost to no one."

E, come già se' de' miei rari amici,
Donna vedrai per segno,
Che farà gli occhi tuoi via piú felici. —

I' volea dir — Quest' è impossibil cosa —;
Quand' ella — Or mira (e leva' gli occhi un poco)
In piú riposto loco
Donna ch' a pochi si mostrò già mai. —
Ratto inchinai la fronte vergognosa
Sentendo novo dentro maggior foco:
Et ella il prese in gioco,
Dicendo — I' veggio ben dove tu stai.
Sí come 'l sol con suoi possenti rai
Fa súbito sparire ogni altra stella,
Cosi par or men bella
La vista mia cui maggior luce preme.
Ma io però da' miei non ti diparto:
Ché questa e me d'un seme,
Lei d'avanti e me poi, produsse un parto. —

Ruppesi in tanto di vergogna il nodo
Ch' a la mia lingua era distretto intorno
Su nel primiero scorno
Allor quand' io del suo accorger m'accorsi;
E 'ncominciai — S' egli è ver quel ch' i' odo
Beato il padre e benedetto il giorno
C' ha di voi 'l mondo adorno
E tutto 'l tempo ch' a vedervi io corsi!
E, se mai da la via dritta mi torsi,
Duolmene forte assai piú ch' io non mostro
Ma, se de l'esser vostro
Fossi degno udir piú, del desir ardo. —

I lifted my eyes
And saw her standing surrounded by dark silences.

My head bent down. A new shame clenched in my heart.
My lady spoke almost as if she were amused.
"I understand you. As the sun with its powerful
Light makes every other star suddenly go blank,
So now the lesser beauty of my face
Is vanquished by a greater beauty.
You may remain my servant even with this knowledge.
We are of the same seed, and of a single birth,
She the first born."
Her understanding allowed my shame some motion.
It had been her scorn that bound me,
Had kept me speechless. "I bless the father,
I bless the day that graced the earth with your presence.
The time that I have spent seeking for you,
If I have stepped from your following
Or your example, ever, I grieve greatly,
More than I have shown. I wish to know
More of you, if I am worth it."

I felt her understanding penetrate my body
With her speech. "As pleased our eternal father,
Each of us was born immortal.
It would have been easier for you had he not made us.
Love, beauty, youth and light
We sometimes were, and now we are come to this,
That she beats her wings
To turn to her ancient covert;
And I am my own shadow only, that is all."
Then moving briefly toward me, she said,

Pensosa mi rispose; e così fiso
Tenne il suo dolce sguardo,
Ch' al cor mandò co le parole il viso.

— Sí come piacque al nostro eterno padre,
Ciascuna di noi due nacque immortale.
Miseri! a voi che vale?
Me' v'era che da noi fosse 'l defetto.
Amate, belle, giovani e leggiadre
Fummo alcun tempo; et or siam giunte a tale,
Che costei batte l'ale
Per tornar a l'antico suo ricetto;
I' per me son un' ombra. Et or t' ho detto
Quanto per te sí breve intender puossi. —
Poi che i piè suoi fûr mossi,
Dicendo — Non temer ch' i' m'allontani —,
Di verde lauro una ghirlanda colse,
La qual co le sue mani
Intorno intorno a le mie tempie avolse.

Canzon; chi tua ragion chiamasse oscura,
Di': Non ho cura, — perché tosto spero
Ch' altro messaggio il vero
Farà in piú chiara voce manifesto.
I' venni sol per isvegliare altrui;
Se chi m'impose questo
Non m'ingannò quand' io parti' da lui.

"Don't be afraid at my going away."
And, taking a garland from a green laurel
With her hands
She wound, wound it around my temples.

I am a song woven of darkness.
Truth follows after in a plain voice.
My coming is to be the wakening.
My maker willed that when he cut me loose.

Quel vago impallidir, che 'l dolce riso
D'un'amorosa nebbia ricoperse,
Con tanta maestade al cor s'offerse,
Che li si fece incontr' a mezzo 'l viso.

Conobbi allor sí come in paradiso
Vede l'un l'altro; in tal guisa s'aperse
Quel pietoso penser, ch' altri non scerse,
Ma vidil' io, ch' altrove non m'affiso.

Ogni angelica vista, ogni atto umile,
Che già mai in donna, ov' amor fusse, apparve,
Fôra uno sdegno a lato a quel ch' i' dico.

Chinava a terra il bel guardo gentile,
E tacendo dicea com' a me parve:
Chi m'allontana il mio fedele amico?

Color drained from her face. She smiled
With some effort. My own love answered smiling.

I knew how people see each other after they die:
The simplicity of kind knowledge. I saw it.
I was ready to see such a thing.

And what I saw makes kindliness
Or grace, in any other woman where love is,
Seem paltry, seem a gesture of scorn.

She turned her face to the ground, silently
Asking, "Who has drawn my friend so far from me?"

Chiare, fresche e dolci acque,
Ove le belle membra
Pose colei che sola a me par donna;
Gentil ramo, ove piacque
(Con sospir mi rimembra)
A lei di fare al bel fianco colonna;
Erba e fior che la gonna
Leggiadra ricoverse
Co l' angelico seno;
Aer sacro sereno,
Ove Amor co' begli occhi il cor m'aperse;
Date udïenza insieme
A le dolenti mie parole estreme.

S' egli è pur mio destino,
E 'l cielo in ciò s'adopra,
Ch' Amor quest' occhi lagrimando chiuda;
Qualche grazia il meschino
Corpo fra voi ricopra,
E torni l'alma al proprio albergo ignuda.
La morte fia men cruda,
Se questa spene porto
A quel dubbioso passo;
Ché lo spirito lasso
Non poria mai 'n piú riposato porto
Né in piú tranquilla fossa
Fuggir la carne travagliata e l'ossa.

126

Biting bright water,
The lovely flesh of her
Rests in the chill current.
This branch sprang back with the weight of her
Side pressed in among leaves;
And her gown shadowed an instant,
And covered, grass and the tiny flowers,
Shadowed her breasts.
And the air sacred, calmed.
My heart burst open.
This is the last thing I will say.

It is the decision of the wise stars
That love close my eyes with weeping.
With your grace let my sad
Body be covered with earth in this place,
My soul go naked to its proper home.
Death will come with more ease,
May I be assured that my soul
In its dangerous passage
Abandon the worked flesh and bone
To a grave place so peaceful.

Tempo verrà ancor forse
Ch' a l'usato soggiorno
Torni la fera bella e mansueta,
E là, 'v' ella mi scòrse
Nel benedetto giorno,
Volga la vista disïosa e lieta,
Cercandomi; et, o pièta!,
Già terra in fra le pietre
Vedendo, Amor l'inspiri
In guisa, che sospiri
Sí dolcemente che mercé m'impetre
E faccia forza al cielo
Asciugandosi gli occhi co 'l bel velo.

Da' be' rami scendea,
(Dolce ne la memoria)
Una pioggia di fior sovra 'l suo grembo;
Et ella si sedea
Umile in tanta gloria,
Coverta già de l'amoroso nembo.
Qual fior cadea su 'l lembo,
Qual su le treccie bionde,
Ch' oro forbito e perle
Eran quel dí a vederle;
Qual si posava in terra, e qual su l'onde;
Qual con un vago errore
Girando parea dir — Qui regna Amore —.

And then, after a waiting,
The time might come, some time,
When gentleness tames her fierce scorn
And she will come again to this place,
Searching for me: will find me earth under stone.
Knowing love for me, finding mercy,
She would begin to teach the stars new patterns.

And memory vanishing will allow this
Branch free motion, and with a sweep
It showers her with blossoms.
And while she sits there, the clouds
Of flowers swirl around her, falling
On white linen, the braided golden hair,
Warm pearl glancing with gold.
And the earth is heavy with blossoms, the water
Heavy with the scent and the lost petals.
Love lives still. I am afraid. She is not mortal.

Quante volte diss' io
Allor pien di spavento
— Costei per fermo nacque in paradiso —:
Cosí carco d'obblio,
Il divin portamento
E 'l volto e le parole e 'l dolce riso
M'aveano, e sí diviso
Da l'imagine vera,
Ch' i' dicea sospirando
— Qui come venn' io, o quando? —
Credendo esser in ciel, non là dov' era.
Da indi in qua mi piace
Quest' erba sí, ch' altrove non ho pace.

Su tu avessi ornamenti quant' hai voglia,
Potresti arditamente
Uscir del bosco e gir in fra la gente.

And I have lost the truth of the frank image
In vision and bewilderment.
But blessed peace lives in this grassy place,
Lives no place else for me.

Were people so peaceful I would be bold amongst them.

I' vidi in terra angelici costumi
E celesti bellezze al mondo sole;
Tal che di rimembrar mi giova e dole,
Ché quant' io miro par sogni, ombre e fumi.

E vidi lagrimar que' duo bei lumi,
C' han fatto mille volte invidia al sole;
Et udii sospirando dir parole
Che farian gire i monti e stare i fiumi.

Amor, senno, valor, pietate e doglia
Facean piangendo un piú dolce concento
D'ogni altro che nel mondo udir si soglia;

Ed era il cielo a l'armonia sí 'ntento,
Che non si vedea 'n ramo mover foglia;
Tanta dolcessa avea pien l'aere e 'l vento!

156

I saw the tracks of angels in the earth,
The beauty of heaven walking by itself on the world.
Joke or sorrow now, it seems a dream
Shadow, or smoke.

I saw a kind of rain that made the sun ashamed,
And heard her, speaking sad words, make mountains
Shift, the rivers stop.

Love, wisdom, valor, pity, pain,
Made better harmony with weeping
Than any other likely to be heard in the world.

And the air and the wind were so filled with this deep music
No single leaf moved on its still branch.

162

Lieti fiori e felici e ben nate erbe
Che Madonna pensando premer sòle;
Piaggia ch' ascolti sue dolci parole,
E del bel piede alcun vestigio serbe;

Schietti arboscelli e verdi frondi acerbe;
Amorosette e pallide vïole;
Ombrose selve, ove percote il sole
Che vi fa co' suoi raggi alte e superbe;

O soave contrada, o puro fiume
Che bagni il suo bel viso e gli occhi chiari
E prendi qualità dal vivo lume:

Quanto v'invidio gli atti onesti e cari!
Non fia in voi scoglio omai che per costume
D'arder co la mia fiamma non impari.

When she walks by here
The grass bends down, the gentle flowers.
The mark of her foot remains in the damp ground beside water.

You have known her, the slenderness of trees,
Young green branches: making a shadowy wood
The sun breaks with its narrow shafts of gold smoke.

River, that has become her face, takes fire
Looking at me; fire from the sun has washed her.

The stones themselves are burning in my shadow.

164

Or che 'l ciel e la terra e 'l vento tace
E le fere e gli augelli il sonno affrena,
Notte il carro stellato in giro mena
E nel suo letto il mar senz' onda giace;

Vegghio, penso, ardo, piango; e chi mi sface
Sempre m'è inanzi per mia dolce pena:
Guerra è 'l mio stato, d'ira e di duol piena;
E sol di lei pensando ho qualche pace.

Cosí sol d'una chiara fonte viva
Move 'l dolce e l'amaro ond' io mi pasco;
Una man sola mi risana e punge.

E perché 'l mio martír non giunga a riva,
Mille volte il dí moro e mille nasco;
Tanto da la salute mia son lunge.

Now silence. Earth and wind,
Wild animals, birds—sleep takes them in.
Night turns the wheel full of stars,
And the sea, motionless in its deep bed.

My awareness burns. I keep my eyes open.
I have grown into war. Her image
Sings sweetness into the eternal pain.
Anger and grief know only this much peace.

Sweet water feeds my mouth with bitterness;
Her healing hand causes new wounding.

Life and death are balanced evenly in my time for now,
So far am I from my salvation.

Po, ben puo'tu portartene la scorza
Di me con tue possenti e rapide onde;
Ma lo spirto ch' iv' entro si nasconde
Non cura né di tua né d'altrui forza:

Lo qual, senz' alternar poggia con òrza,
Dritto per l'aure al suo desir seconde,
Battendo l'ali verso l'aurea fronde,
L'acqua e' l vento e la vela e i remi sforza.

Re de gli altri, superbo, altero fiume,
Che 'ncontri 'l sol quando e' ne mena il girono
E 'n ponente abandoni un piú bel lume,

Tu te ne vai co 'l mio mortal su 'l corno:
L'altro coverto d'amorose piume
Torna volando al suo dolce soggiorno.

180

You can carry my husk of body off,
River. My soul has no sense of your power,
Nor any other.

It will take the wind face to face,
All air and hollow bone, to the golden branch.
Desire survives strong water.

King river, when you meet the sun bringing day
You leave a fairer light abandoned.

You can take only my mortal flesh into your house.
That other soars to its dipping branch.

Almo sol, quella fronde ch' io sola amo
Tu prima amasti: or sola al bel soggiorno
Verdeggia, e senza par, poi che l'adorno
Suo male e nostro vide in prima Adamo.

Stiamo a mirarla: i' ti pur prego e chiamo,
O sole; e tu pur fuggi, e fai d'intorno
Ombrare i poggi, e te ne porti il giorno,
E fuggendo mi tôi quel ch' i' piú bramo.

L'ombra che cade da quell' umil colle
Ove favilla il mio soave foco,
Ove 'l gran lauro fu picciola verga,

Crescendo mentr' io parlo, a gli occhi tolle
La dolce vista del beato loco
Ove il mio cor co la sua donna alberga.

You were this tree's first lover, sun;
Tree whom I love now; and kept her loveliness
Green always, unequalled since Adam's sin
Stood out clearly before us.

We will look at it together.
Yet you leave my prayer in the shadow of hills
Lengthening; take daylight and my vision.

The shadow falling from the low hill
Where my bright flare gleams,
Where the great laurel was a frail sapling,

Growing while I speak, invades my eyes,
Darkens the dwelling where her brightness was,
Takes my heart's shelter.

Stiamo, Amor, a veder la gloria nostra,
Cose sopra natura, altere e nove:
Vedi ben quanta in lei dolcezza piove;
Vedi lume che 'l cielo in terra mostra.

Vedi quant'arte dora e 'mperla e 'nostra
L' abito eletto e mai non visto altrove,
Che dolcemente i piedi e gli occhi move
Per questa di bei colli ombrosa chiostra.

L'erbetta verde e i fior di color mille
Sparsi sotto quell'elce antiqua e negra
Pregan pur che 'l bel piè li prema o tócchi:

E 'l ciel di vaghe e lucide faville
S'accende in torno, e 'n vista si rallegra
D'esser fatto seren da sí belli occhi.

192

Love, let us wait to watch our glory:
Things high and new over nature.
You see how sweetness showers on her,
See the light heaven casts over the land.

Through this shadow, enclosed by hills,
How gently she moves her mask
Of crimson clothing, gold.

Each sprig of grass, the thousand bright
Flowers scattered in shadow under the stooped oak
Beg the weight of her walking.

And heaven, pierced with sharp stars,
Burns with desire, makes itself altogether new;
Makes itself clear and brilliant.

Rapido fiume, che d'alpestra vena,
Rodendo intorno, onde 'l tuo nome prendi,
Notte e dí meco disïoso scendi
Ov' Amor me, te sol Natura mena;

Vattene innanzi: il tuo corso non frena
Né stanchezza né sonno: e pria che rendi
Suo dritto al mar, fiso, u' si mostri, attendi
L'erba piú verde e l'aria piú serena.

Ivi è quel nostro vivo e dolce sole
Ch' adorna e 'nfiora la tua riva manca;
Forse (oh che spero?) il mio tardar le dole.

Basciale 'l piede o la man bella e bianca:
Dille (el basciar sia 'n vece di parole)
— Lo spirto è pronto, ma la carne è stanca. —

Snow has learned swiftness and roared out of the mountains.
Your channel follows my desire.
Let your loud water learn my love also.

Water does not sleep, nor weary.
But with my nature bound in yours, before the sea
Takes its justice, we will rest a moment in calm air.

There is a sun who lives among flowers on your left bank.
She will look down and see my face.
She will wonder at my lateness.

We will kiss her foot then, and the warm flesh of her hand . . .

I dolci colli, ov' io lasciai me stesso
Partendo onde partir già mai non posso,
Mi vanno innanzi; ed èmmi ogni or a dosso
Quel caro peso ch' Amor m' ha commesso.

Meco di me mi meraviglio spesso,
Ch' i' pur vo sempre, e non son ancor mosso
Dal bel giogo piú volte indarno scosso,
Ma com' piú me n'allungo e piú m'appresso.

E, qual cervo ferito di saetta
Co 'l ferro avelenato dentr' al fianco
Fugge, e piú duolsi quanto piú s'affretta,

Tal io con quello stral dal lato manco,
Che mi consuma e parte mi diletta,
Di duol mi struggo e di fuggir mi stanco.

209

I have pretended a banishment I cannot master.
The weight of love in me has printed the gentle hills.
I am hemmed in there.

I am amazed that my long walks take me no distance.
I am leashed back like an animal in training,
Walk in circles.

The frantic deer frets the arrow deeper,
Poisonous in his side, the more he fights
The closing trees.

I feel the same wound in my left side.
I confess the lines of pain give me some pleasure.

Voglia mi sprona, Amor mi guida e scorge,
Piacer mi tira, usanza mi trasporta,
Speranza mi lusinga e riconforta
E la man destra al cor già stanco porge.

El misero la prende e non s'accorge
Di nostra cieca e disleale scorta:
Regnano i sensi, e la ragion è morta:
De l'un vago desio l'altro risorge.

Vertute, onor, bellezza, atto gentile,
Dolci parole a i be' rami m' han giunto,
Ove soavemente il cor s'invesca.

Mille trecento ventisette, a punto
Su l'ora prima il dí sesto d'aprile,
Nel laberinto intrai; né veggio ond' esca.

Wish spurs me on. Love looks and nods.
Pleasure drags me. Old habit carries,
Hope flatters and recomforts me, and offers
Its right hand to a heart already viciously tired.

And, taken in once more
By the easy blindness my guide offers
I have hope again. Desire breeds desire.
The senses rule over a dead mind.

Strength, honor, beauty, gentle gestures,
Fair speech—I have woven my heart
Into this net of branches, with comfort and deliberation.

In the year 1327, at the opening of the first hour,
On the sixth of April, I entered the labyrinth.
My wandering since has been without purpose.

Il cantar novo e 'l pianger de li augelli
In su 'l dí fanno retentir le valli,
E 'l mormorar de' liquidi cristalli
Giú per lucidi freschi rivi e snelli.

Quella c' ha neve il volto, oro i capelli,
Nel cui amor non fûr mai inganni né falli,
Destami al suon de li amorosi balli,
Pettinando al suo vecchio i bianchi velli.

Cosí mi sveglio a salutar l'aurora
E 'l sol ch' è seco, e piú l'altro ond' io fui
Ne' primi anni abagliato e son ancora.

I' gli ho veduti alcun giorno ambedui
Levarsi inseme, e 'n un punto e 'n un'ora
Quel far le stelle e questo sparir lui.

The new song and weeping of birds
At the beginning of day, makes the valley ring.
Fresh crystal hums through light, brisk rivers.

She whose face is snow, golden haired,
Whose love has never held deceit,
Wakes me, moving the whole sky in her dance.
She allows her fingers to part the white wool of her old lover.

I wake this way, and salute the dawn,
And the sun that is with her—and then that other sun
Who made a barrier of gold before my eyes.

I have seen, some days, both
Rise together—and at a single instant
One make the stars, the other the sun vanish.

223

Quando 'l sol bagna in mar l'aurato carro
E l'aere nostro e la mia mente imbruna,
Co 'l cielo e co le stelle e co la luna
Un'angosciosa e dura notte innarro.

Poi, lasso!, a tal che non m'ascolta narro
Tutte le mie fatiche ad una ad una,
E co 'l mondo e con mia cieca fortuna,
Con Amor, con Madonna e meco garro.

Il sonno è 'n bando, e del riposo è nulla;
Ma sospiri e lamenti in fin a l'alba,
E lagrime che l'alma a li occhi invia.

Vien poi l'aurora, e l'aura fosca inalba,
Me no: ma 'l sol che 'l cor m'arde e trastulla,
Quel po solo adolcir la doglia mia.

223

When the sun bathes its golden car in the sea,
And our day, and my mind, darken,
I embark on the night's anguish.

My audience does not know I am speaking;
My audience being my pain—the world, blind
Fate, love, lady, my self rebuking.

I watch my tears stand out against the darkness.
In such a way my soul makes itself visible to me.

Dawn rises. Lightness comes over the sky.
The shadow does not leave me.
My heart rejoices in the great burning.

Cantai, or piango, e non men di dolcezza
Del pianger prendo che del canto presi;
Ch' a la cagion, non a l'effetto, intesi
Son i miei sensi vaghi pur d'altezza.

Indi e mansüetudine e durezza
Et atti feri et umili e cortesi
Porto egualmente; né me gravan pesi,
Né l'arme mie punta di sdegni spezza.

Tengan dunque vèr' me l'usato stile
Amor, madonna, il mondo e mia fortuna;
Ch' i' non penso esser mai se non felice.

Viva o mora o languisca, un piú gentile
Stato del mio non è sotto la luna;
Sí dolce è del mio amaro la radice!

The root of my bitterness is sweet.
The moon has not presided over a country gentle
To my living or my death. I claim this one.

Events keep their usual course to me;
My love, she whom I love.
What comes to me must be happy in some way.

Disdain has not broken my shield;
Nor does the weight of my invention crush me—
Fierce gestures of polite humility, meekly
Executed by pain.

I sang once. My weeping carries as much sweetness.
It is the high cause that my senses long for.
My misery is a minor end.

O cameretta, che già fosti un porto
A le gravi tempeste mie dïurne,
Fonte se' or di lagrime notturne
Che 'l dí celate per vergogna porto!

O letticciuol, che requie eri e conforto
In tanti affanni, di che dogliose urne
Ti bagna Amor con quelle mani eburne
Solo vèr' me crudeli a sí gran torto!

Né pur il mio secreto e 'l mio riposo
Fuggo, ma piú me stesso e 'l mio pensero,
Che, seguendo 'l, tal or levommi a volo;

E 'l vulgo, a me nemico et odïoso,
(Chi 'l pensò mai?) per mio refugio chero:
Tal paura ho di ritrovarmi solo.

I inhabit a small room. It is shaking
With storms I thought to hide from.
I carry them with me, then.

My bed moves like a sea,
Harboring its own grief.

I escape my privacy, leave behind me
There myself, my stunted thinking.

I am so terrified of being alone
I catch myself arranging encounters with milkmen,
Civil servants, the people who sell vegetables.

L'aura, che 'l verde lauro e l'aureo crine
Soavemente sospirando move,
Fa con sue viste leggiadrette e nove
L'anime da' lor corpi pellegrine.

Candida rosa nata in dure spine,
Quando fia chi sua pari al mondo trove?
Gloria di nostra etate! O vivo Giove,
Manda, prego, il mio in prima che 'l suo fine:

Sí ch' io non veggia il gran publico danno,
E 'l mondo remaner senza 'l suo sole,
Né li occhi miei che luce altra non hanno,

Né l'alma, che pensar d'altro non vòle;
Nè l'orecchie, ch' udir altro non sanno,
Senza l'oneste sue dolci parole.

246

Sunlight and shadow moving
With a light wind through these green laurel
Branches, make new sights. The same wind
Takes souls from their bodies.

White rose in wild thicket;
When will her like be seen again in the world?
I am afraid. It should be I who die first.

The world would be wrapped in shadow
Like a corpse at a great public funeral.
I would see nothing any more,

Nor hear, nor allow my soul the movement
Of thought; nor imagine even
The honest life vanishing out of trees
Like desperate pilgrims.

Chi vuol veder quantunque po natura
E 'l ciel tra noi, venga a mirar costei,
Ch' è sola un sol, non pur a li occhi mei
Ma al mondo cieco che vertú non cura;

E venga tosto, perché morte fura
Prima i migliori e lascia star i rei:
Questa, aspettata al regno de li dei,
Cosa bella mortal, passa e non dura.

Vedrà, s'arriva a tempo, ogni vertute,
Ogni bellezza, ogni real costume
Giunti in un corpo con mirabil tempre;

Allor dirà che mie rime son mute,
L'ingegno offeso dal soverchio lume:
Ma, se piú tarda, avrà da pianger sempre.

248

Look at her. You will see nature's power
Hanging like the sun over a blind world.

Quickly. Death searches out the gentlest.
Loveliness is mortal. She is looked for.

He sidles up beside a creature in spring
Temper, everything wonderful in one flesh.

My crazed verse is stricken with sun.
Look on this glare before blindness

Rides weeping over the world.

Qual paura ho quando mi torna a mente
Quel giorno ch' i' lasciai grave e pensosa
Madonna e 'l mio cor seco! e non è cosa
Che sí volentier pensi e sí sovente.

I' la riveggio starsi umilemente
Tra belle donne, a guisa d' una rosa
Tra minor' fior; né lieta né dogliosa,
Come chi teme et altro mal non sente.

Deposta avea l'usata leggiadria,
Le perle e le ghirlande e i panni allegri
E 'l riso e 'l canto e 'l parlar dolce umano.

Cosí in dubbio lasciai la vita mia:
Or tristi auguri e sogni e penser negri,
Mi danno assalto; e piaccia a Dio che 'n vano.

I left a grave lady, thoughtful.
Fear takes my memory. My glad heart
Is still in that place, but fearful now.

I see her standing quietly among fair women,
A rose hung over a daisy bed.
She shows neither joy nor sorrow.
She is afraid only.

She has put away finery: gay cloth,
Green windings of wild branches bound with pearls.
No one is singing. Or she herself is not singing.

I feel my own sad life in the balance.
I cannot shake this black stillness,
This vision.

Solea lontana in sonno consolarme
Con quella dolce angelica sua vista
Madonna; or mi spaventa e mi contrista,
Né di duol né di téma posso aitarme:

Ché spesso nel suo volto veder parme
Vera pietà con grave dolor mista,
Et udir cose onde 'l cor fede acquista
Che di gioia e di speme si disarme.

— Non ti sovèn di quella ultima sera, —
Dice ella, — ch' i' lasciai li occhi tuoi molli,
E sforzata dal tempo me n'andai?

I' non te 'l potei dir allor né volli,
Or te 'l dico per cosa esperta e vera:
Non sperar di vedermi in terra mai.

250

I am awake. She has come to me
In my sleep, as she used to do bringing comfort.
I am left this time with terrified sadness.

Her face was sad. She looked on me with pity.

"Do you remember the last evening
When I left you weeping? I
Had known it was time.

I could not quite tell you then
What must be true—
You will not see me again in the world."

Bibliography

EDITIONS

These translations were made, for the most part, in the winter of 1969. In making these translations I worked from the edition of Giosué Carducci and S. Ferrari, *Le Rime di Francesco Petrarca,* published by Sansoni in Florence, 1899, and reprinted by Sansoni with an introduction by Gianfranco Contini in 1957.

We have felt it best to reproduce, as our Italian text, the actual one from which these versions were originally made.

Other editions available include:

Contini, Gianfranco, ed. *Canzoniere.* Annotated by Daniele Ponchiroli, 3rd ed. Turin: Einaudi, 1964.

Griffith, T. Gwynfor, and Hainsworth, P. R. J., eds. *Petrarch: Selected Poems.* Manchester: Manchester University Press, 1971.

Neri, F.; Martellotti, G.; Bianchi, E.; and Sapegno, N.; eds. *Rime, "Trionfi" e poesie latine.* Milan: Ricciardi, 1951.

Of particular usefulness due to its recent availability in paperback is the Italian text included in *Petrarch's Lyric Poems,* translated and edited by Robert M. Durling. Cambridge, Massachusetts: Harvard University Press, 1976.

BIOGRAPHY

Bishop, Morris. *Petrarch and His World.* Bloomington: Indiana University Press, 1963.

Wilkins, Ernest Hatch. *Life of Petrarch.* Chicago: Chicago University Press, 1961.

SELECTIONS AND ANTHOLOGIES

Bergin, Thomas Goddard, ed. *Petrarch, Selected Sonnets, Odes and Letters.* Arlington Heights, Illinois: AHM Publishing Corporation, 1966.

Bishop, Morris, ed. and trans. *Letters from Petrarch.* Bloomington: Indiana University Press, 1966.

Robinson, J. H. and Rolfe, H. W. *Petrarch: The First Modern Scholar and Man of Letters.* 2nd ed. New York: Putnam, 1914.

Thompson, David B., ed. and trans. *Petrarch, a Humanist among Princes: An Anthology of Petrarch's Letters and of Selections from His Other Works.* New York: Harper & Row, 1971.

Wilkins, Ernest Hatch, trans. *Petrarch at Vaucluse: Letters in Verse and Prose.* Chicago: University of Chicago Press, 1958.

RECENT ENGLISH TRANSLATIONS

Armi, Anna Maria, trans. *Petrarch's Sonnets and Songs.* New York: Pantheon, 1946.

Auslander, Joseph, trans. *The Sonnets of Petrarch.* London: Longmans, Green, 1931.

Bergin, Thomas Goddard, ed. *The Rhymes of Francesco Petrarca: A Selection of Translations.* Edinburgh: Oliver and Boyd, 1954.

Bergin, Thomas Goddard, trans. *The Sonnets of Petrarch, Together with English Translations.* Verona: Limited Editions, 1965.

Bishop, Morris, trans. *Love Rhymes of Petrarch.* Ithaca, N.Y.: Dragon Press, 1932.

Durling, Robert M. *Petrarch's Lyric Poems.* Cambridge, Mass.: Harvard University Press, 1976.

Mortimer, Anthony, *Petrarch: Selected Poems.* Alabama: University of Alabama Press, 1977.

Design by David Bullen
Typeset in Mergenthaler Sabon
by Robert Sibley
Printed by Maple-Vail
on acid-free paper